99 FACTS ABOUT FARTS - THE ULTIMATE FUN FACT BOOK

J.N. Storm

ISBN-13: 978-1519246677

ISBN-10: 1519246676

For any questions or requests, write to: post@funfactbooks.com

"You don't have to be smart to laugh at farts, but you'd have to be stupid not to."
--Jon Stewart

CONTENT

PREFACE

Dear Reader,

Let's make one thing clear right from the start - farts *are* the funniest thing in the world!

I fart, you fart, we all fart! But there's probably a lot about farting that you might not know. Here's the book that gives you 99 amazing, awesome, fascinating and hilarious facts about farts.

Reading is important for us and for many reasons. It empowers us with knowledge, it relieves stress, and it improves our memory and stimulates our brain just to mention some. And, it can be a lot of fun too!

Thank you for purchasing 99 Facts About Farts. For me it was the funniest project I have ever worked on and I hope you have a lot of fun reading it.

J.N. Storm

PS: Are you and your kids up for a challenge? Get your FREE copy of the "The Ultimate Quiz Book About Farts". Visit funfactbooks.com/free-quiz-book. It will have you all laughing out loud!

CHAPTER ONE

The Word Fart

Definition

Fart fact # 1

According to www.thefreedictionary.com the definition of a fart is "To expel intestinal gas through the anus".

Origin of the word

Fart fact # 2

Fart is one of the oldest words in the English lexicon.

According to British Dictionary the word fart[1] originates from Middle English *farten*; related to Old Norse *freta*, Old High German *ferzan* (to break wind), Sanskrit pardatē (he breaks wind).

The negative associations[2] to the word seem to have come about towards the late 19th Century when it was used in a personal context, as in "you old fart" etc.

---

[1] http://dictionary.reference.com/browse/fart
[2] http://dictionary.reference.com/browse/fart

Medical term

Fart fact # 3

The medical term for a fart is *flatulence.*

The scientific study of *flatulence* is termed *flatology* (yes, someone does actually study farts!)

CHAPTER TWO

Fart Statistics and More

Amount of farts per day

Fart fact # 4

The average person farts between 10 and 20 times per day, and on average about 14 times per day.

Amount of farts in a lifetime

Fart fact # 5

The average person will release half a million farts in their lifetime!

Total amount of farts every day

Fart fact # 6

More than 1.15 million farts happen every second on earth! That's one hundred billion human farts every day. Whoa that's a whole lot of farts!

Amount of farts produced

Fart fact # 7

The average person produces about 0.1 to 0.4 gallons[1] of gas per day.

That's 9.41 million gallons[2] of human farts released into our atmosphere every day!

---

[1] 0.5 to 1.5 liters
[2] 3.6 billion liters

Energy produced by a fart

Fart fact # 8

One fart can keep a 60 watt light bulb lit for one second.

If a person were to fart continuously for about seven years[1], or if every person on earth would contribute ten farts each, they would produce enough gas to put a space shuttle into orbit! Those amounts of farts are also more or less the equivalent energy of an atomic bomb!

---

[1] Calculation by jondalar469

The temperature of a fart

Fart fact # 9

The temperature of a freshly formed fart is the same as your body temperature: 98.6 degrees Fahrenheit[1].

See also fart fact Farting in cold weather.

---

[1] 37 degrees Celsius

Afterlife

Fart fact # 10

You'll fart after you die.

Due to gas escaping your digestive tract you will fart for up to three hours after you are dead.

Farts and gender

Fart fact # 11

Men and women are just as gassy (yes, women fart just as much as men).

However, some women experience more gas (and abdominal bloating) during their menstrual cycle, due to changes in hormone levels.

Morning Thunder

Fart fact # 12

Men are most likely to fart first thing in the
morning. It is commonly released in the bathroom and
when achieving good resonance this is known as the
"morning thunder".

Babies and farting

Fart fact # 13

Unborn babies do not fart.

The bacteria which causes digestive gas is not present in an unborn baby and there is no air or oxygen (except for oxygen that is in the blood via the umbilical cord).

CHAPTER THREE

The Chemistry of Farts

Gases in a fart

Fart fact # 14

An average fart is made of:
59 % nitrogen
21% hydrogen
9 % carbon dioxide
7 % methane
4 % oxygen
1 % hydrogen sulfide

We produce much more gas than we realize and one reason is that nearly all of it is odorless. 99 percent of the gas you produce does not smell.

The potent stink is mainly due to the 1 percent of hydrogen sulfide!

Methane

Fart fact # 15

There is only a 50 percent chance that your fart contains methane.

About half of us don't have methane in our farts. Whether you do depends on the kind of organisms living in your intestines.

The color of farts

Fart fact # 16

Farts are colorless.

All the gases that make up a fart have no inherent color.

Fart vs Burp

Fart fact # 17

A burp emerges from the stomach and has a different chemical composition from a fart. Farts have less atmospheric gas content and more bacterial gas content than burps.

Waste

Fart fact # 18

You have 37.2 trillion cells in your body, but more than 10 times that amount of bacteria (and yeast)! Most of them hang out in your digestive tract, living on undigested food that ends up in your lower intestines. They produce your farts as a by-product as they break down food.

Are you healthy?

Fart fact # 19

Farting proves you are healthy!

A fart is the result of a healthy, complex ecosystem in your intestines. So it is reason to say that it's unfortunate that we, in our modern society, consider farting negative.

But, if you fart multiple times each hour it might be because you are experiencing an inability to digest some kinds of dairy products (lactose intolerance).

Starving your farts

Fart fact # 20

Even though it is possible, starving your fart-producing bacteria is not a good idea.

The amount you produce is the result of both your balance of gut bacteria and your diet, and it is not recommended to try mess with it.

Foods that make smelly farts

Fart fact # 21

Hydrogen sulfide makes farts smell like rotten eggs and this comes from the natural bacterial breakdown of organic matter.

But what we eat matters when it comes to how smelly our farts are.

Foods containing sulfur such as cabbage, kale and even meat and eggs make farts more smellier. Also a diet full of complex carbohydrates such as potatoes, and foods rich in fiber, such as beans and whole grain affects our farting.

Methanethiol makes farts smell putrid and is found in foods like nuts and cheese.

Dimethyl sulfide makes farts smell sweet and is found in foods such as cabbage and seafood.

Gum and soda

Fart fact # 22

They can make you fart more!

Apart from the gases produced by bacteria, a significant proportion of your farts are simply made up of air being swallowed. Some of this swallowing goes on while you're asleep, but it can be increased by drinking beverages and chewing gum. It doesn't smell since it's mostly nitrogen and oxygen. But it sounds and feels the same on exit.

Smoking too, increases farting. The reasons are unknown, but probably just like chewing gum or drinking beverages; smoking makes you swallow more air.

Enjoying the smell

Fart fact # 23

Enjoying the smell of your fart?

When we fart we often think, at least subconsciously, "Wow, I made that!".

Can't smell it?

Fart fact # 24

Your own farts just don't have the same impact on you!

There's a simple reason why you might not mind the smell of your own fart. It might be you even can't even smell it.

You become used to smells over time. Ever noticed a scent walking into a stranger's house, but seldom in your own? You get used to smells and so also the characteristic mix of odors' produced by your bacteria that differ slightly from everybody else's.

Filtering farts

Fart fact # 25

Farts can, to some extent be filtered through your underwear (or clothing).

Filtering would in such a case mean that some particles pass through, while others get trapped in your underwear (see fart fact Smelly Fingers).
For more on this topic see the facts about Fart Pants and Shreddies.

Inhaling farts

Fart fact # 26

If you inhale farts they would go into the lungs and simply be exhaled again.

If you for some reason wanted to benefit from other people's farts in order to try and make your own farts smell even worse, you would have to figure out a way to swallow them in order to get them into your digestive system.

Intoxication

Fart fact # 27

Farts are not intoxicating. But most farts contain very little oxygen and you can experience dizziness if you are inhaling high concentrations of farts, simply from the lack of oxygen.

On the other hand, if you are inhaling farts in open air and are breathing rapidly in order to inhale as many farts as possible, you may be hyperventilating, which also makes you feel dizzy.

Where does it go?

Fart fact # 28

Once a clean fart is emitted, it disperses into the atmosphere and does not form into any solid or liquid matter.

However, fine aerosolized particles of liquid and solid poop can condense on surfaces. Most of these particles are polar (with a positively and a negatively charged end) and are therefore attracted to other polar substances or charged surfaces, like a monitor screen (see fart fact Smelly Fingers).

Other fart particles condense on microscopic water droplets in the air if the humidity is very high (as in a bathroom), and some particles go into solution in water.

Farting in the shower

Fart fact # 29

There are several factors why farts smell worse in a shower (or in the bathtub) than anywhere else. First of all, a shower is a small, enclosed space, so the fart gas is more concentrated, and the gas circulates through the shower effectively.

Secondly, the high humidity and high temperature conditions in the shower enhance your sense of smell and taste. The farts don't actually smell worse; it's just that we can smell them more than usual.

Smelly fingers

Fart fact # 30

Your fingers can smell like farts!

A fart can be regarded as "aerosolized poop," which means that microscopic particles of poop are actually distributed throughout the gaseous matrix of the fart. When delivered with some force, the components of the fart can penetrate one's clothing and these tiny particles can be trapped in the fibers of the cloth. The particles are transferred to your fingers and then your nose when you scratch and sniff.

The burning sensation!

Fart fact # 31

The burning sensation that sometimes accompanies a fart is most often caused by a meal of hot peppers or other hot spices. It is actually the oils associated with these foods that remain intact and active all the way through your digestive tract.

Farting in cold weather

Fart fact # 32

You can see your fart in the cold!

When it is cold outside and you fart, you can see it like you can see your breath since farts hold the same temperature as your body on exit.

Freezing a fart

Fart fact # 33

You could freeze a fart!

All it takes is methane under pressure, in the presence of cold water (40 degrees Fahrenheit[1]). The water vapor component of a fart would freeze quite easily, but to freeze the entire fart would require high pressure and low temperature conditions, such as that used to produce dry ice. The fart's composition is unchanged by the process so it will still be smelly when reversed to the gaseous state.

------

[1] 4 degrees Celsius.

Non-lethal

Fart fact # 34

A fart cannot kill you.

Farting doesn't cause tissue damage, it's a medical fact. Fortunately!

Cure for cancer

Fart fact # 35

Farts might cure cancer[1]!

It's the hydrogen sulfide gas, that is naturally produced in our body, that could have significant health benefits!
Small doses can reduce risks for cancer, strokes and more, by preserving structures within our cells.

---

[1] http://www.dailymail.co.uk/health/article-2687696/Could-smelling-farts-GOOD-Potent-gas-flatulence-help-prevent-cancer-strokes-heart-attacks-claims-scientists.html

CHAPTER FOUR

The Physics of Farts

Fart art

Fart fact # 36

Fart's and poop's are end-members of the same process in your digestive tract. You can have pure farts, pure poops, or anything in-between depending on the mixture of the two.

When a fart contains a mixture of only a small amount of poop, well then you get what is known as *fart art* (also known as *skid marks*).

Fart art is most likely to occur if a person is suffering from diarrhea (then pressure against the sphincter is often mistakenly perceived to be gas pressure rather than liquid pressure) or if a person is trying too hard to fart!

Fart art should not be mistaken for what could be the result of inadequate wiping. Inadequate wiping leads to long narrow marks parallel to one's crack, usually with well-defined edges, whereas fart art is generally more circular and has an air-brushed look.

Silent farts

Fart fact # 37

Silent farts often smell way worse than loud ones! This is because they contain less air and therefore a higher concentration of hydrogen sulfide (the smelly gas).

Fart Sounds

Fart fact # 38

The sound of a fart is determined by two factors: muscle and speed.

Less air makes less speed and less sound. With less air there is less vibration on exit.

More air makes it possible to have more speed. If such a fart is not let out slowly it will often be rather loud.

Farts on fire!

Fart fact # 39

You can light a fart on fire!

Since farts contain hydrogen and methane that are both flammable gasses, farts can be set on fire.

Warning: DO NOT try this at home due to a risk of severe injury.

Exploding farts

Fart fact # 40

During a colonoscopy (a medical examination of the colon through the anus) stomach gases have led to explosions! Needless to say, "Colonic gas explosions[1]" as they are called are a frightening medical complication. Good to know they are very rare.

---

[1] http://io9.com/5945897/sometimes-people-explode-during-colonoscopies-heres-how-that-happens?trending_test_c&utm_expid=66866090-62.H_y_0o51QhmMY_tue7bevQ.3&utm_referrer=http%3A%2F%2Fio9.com%2F5945897%2Fsometimes-people-explode-during-colonoscopies-heres-how-that-happens

Holding in a fart

Fart fact # 41

You thought you could hold in a fart?

No, not possible. You can't hold in a fart until it disappears. It might seem to disappear, but it actually doesn't. You just stop being aware of it, but it leaks out gradually. A fart is a bubble of gas and there's nowhere for it to go besides out of your anus.

Speed of a fart

Fart fact # 42

Gas travels at 10 feet per second[1]!

That's the reason you smell a fart in a room even if someone is sitting on the other side.

If you ever wondered - a fart in space would not provide enough thrust to propel you anywhere.

---

[1] 11 kilometers per hour

Traveling direction

Fart fact # 43

Another thing you might have wondered about is why farts travel downward toward the anus when gas has a lower density than liquids and solids, and should therefore travel upwards (that is if you are in an upright position)?

The intestine squeezes its contents toward the anus. The process is stimulated by eating, which is why we often need to poop and fart right after a meal! A zone of high pressure is created, forcing all intestinal contents, gas included, to move towards a region of lower pressure, which is toward the anus.

Optimal farting position

Fart fact # 44

A recent study proved that squatting or moving your thighs against your belly, rather than sitting upright, is the most efficient way to poop. It is probably the best position for farting as well.

Some shift their weight onto one leg and lift the other slightly when farting, but this is probably either to "make way" for the fart or to make their surroundings aware of a fart being imminent.

Storing a fart

Fart fact # 45

Theoretically it's possible to store a fart. But there are some logistical problems and you would need to choose the right kind of container.

A study[1] reported that hydrogen sulfide and other fart gases "rapidly reacted with glass, some plastics, and rubber, but were stable in polypropylene..."

Someone actually tried to make money on storing farts (see fart fact "Fart in a Jar")!

---

[1] Suarez, F.L., J. Springfield, and M.D. Levin (1998) Identification of gasses responsible for the odour of human flatus and evaluation of a device purported to reduce this odour; Gut, v. 43: 100-104.

Ripping of underwear

Fart fact # 46

It is not likely that you will be able to rip your underwear farting (beware, you might instead end up with fart art).

Most underwear is made of material with a fairly high ability to stretch, meaning that it can endure a certain level of extensional force without ripping. Furthermore, much of the fart's force will pass through the spaces rather than stress the fabric.

Stalking farts

Fart fact # 47

Farts follow the farter!

One reason for this annoying characteristic of farts is the turbulence that follows a moving person. The fart is actually pulled along in the farter's direction by the air currents behind the person.

Another reason is that part of the fart is still caught in the farter's clothing, and escapes slowly after the main part of the emission has dispersed.

CHAPTER FIVE

Historical Farts

Oldest joke

Fart fact # 48

Fart jokes have existed for a very long time!

The oldest known joke is some 4,000 years old and it is a Sumerian one-liner: "Something which has never occurred since time immemorial; a young woman did not fart in her husband's lap."

Maybe not the funniest, but it does prove they did think farts were funny, even in ancient times.

Fossil fart

Fart fact # 49

Fossil farts have been discovered to exist!

Scientists have noticed that fossils of a particular species of termite, trapped in amber, were always accompanied by bubbles of gas, analysed to be rich in methane and carbon dioxide.

You can see a photograph of a fossil termite and its farts on the cover of the March 30, 2002 issue of Science News.

17th Earl of Oxford

Fart fact # 50

The 17th Earl of Oxford, Edward de Vere, passed gas as he bowed, while swearing loyalty to Elizabeth I. He was so ashamed he left traveling for seven years! On his return the Queen welcomed him home and said *"My Lord, I had forgotten the fart."*

But what did he do during those seven years? Edward de Vere is one of the people most often mentioned as the potential author of Shakespeare's plays. You might believe it's true when you learn about the jokes in Shakespeare's plays (see fart fact about William Shakespeare).

World War Two

Fart fact # 51

The Air Force[1] estimates that at least one thousand airmen were killed because of farting during World War Two.

Un-pressurized aircrafts, like the B-17 bombers, operating at an altitude of 20,000 feet would cause intestinal gas to expand 300% causing their intestines to rupture.

---

[1] http://world-war-2.info/facts/

First cinematic fart

Fart fact # 52

The movie *Blazing Saddles*[1] from 1974 made movie history in a scene where a gang of bandits are sitting around a camp fire farting. This was the first time audible farts had been heard in a movie theatre, ever!

---

[1] http://mentalfloss.com/article/54636/11-things-you-might-not-know-about-blazing-saddles

CHAPTER SIX

Geographical Farts

Rome

Fart fact # 53

In ancient Rome (some 2,500 years ago) emperor Claudius intended to pass a law[1]: "allowing to all people the liberty of giving vent at table to any distension occasioned by flatulence" fearing that holding farts in is harmful for health.

---

[1] http://ancienthistory.about.com/od/Ancient-Quotes/fl/120613-Emperor-Claudius-on-Farts.htm

Japan

Fart fact # 54

He-Gassen is a Japanese art scroll created some 200 years ago by unknown artists. The scroll is of scenes with characters farting at each other.

It is to be said that the scroll was made to express a political message.

Amazonas

Fart fact # 55

The Yanomami tribe of some 35,000 people living in the Amazonas are said to fart as a means of saying hello!

Malawi

Fart fact # 56

In the African country of Malawi a bill was passed in 2011 that made it illegal to fart! Or at least that became the popular understanding of the law stating that: "Any person who vitiates the atmosphere in any place so as to make it noxious to the public ... shall be guilty of a misdemeanour".

The Minister of Justice George Chaponda said: "Nature can be controlled... it becomes a nuisance if people fart anywhere".

Germany

Fart fact # 57

In 2014 a German farm shed exploded[1]. A static electric charge ignited gas from 90 cows that had been built up in the structure.

One cow was treated for burns.

---

[1] http://www.reuters.com/article/2014/01/27/us-germany-cows-idUSBREA0Q1HY20140127

CHAPTER SEVEN

Farting in Space and Other Environments

Scuba diving

Fart fact # 58

Scuba divers can pass gas at probably any depths, since any gas space in the body when under pressure will be compressed. That is why it is not likely you will feel a need to fart on your way down, as one might think. If you build up gas under pressure however, the situation off course is different. It would expand as you go up and you would definitely need to let go of some gas!

One thing to consider if you are wearing a dry suit; you would probably want to hold any gas in rather than letting it out in your suit to welcome you when you get out of water and open it.

Flying

Fart fact # 59

We fart more when we fly!

High-altitude flatulence has to do with a change in atmospheric pressure and altitude. Airplane cabins are pressurized to be the equivalent to about an 8,000-feet altitude[1] which is quite a significant pressure change for the human body.

When the atmospheric pressure in the cabin decreases, the volume of intestinal gas increases. With a greater volume of intestinal gas it means you're going to pass more of it.

---

[1] http://www.who.int/ith/mode_of_travel/cab/en/

In Space

Fart fact # 60

Flatulence is a normal process, even in space!

"It is an indication of "things to come" just like here on Earth. When your gas starts to stink, and is inhaled by those around you, manners dictate that it's time to find the toilet and perform a "waste dump!" The appearance of a strong and pungent odor was one of my best indicators that it was time for me to go to the bathroom because, in the absence of gravity, "normal" earthbound indicators did not always suffice" explains NASA astronaut Clayton C. Anderson[1].

---

[1] https://www.quora.com/How-do-farts-behave-in-low-gravity/answer/Clayton-C-Anderson

Space stations

Fart fact # 61

In gravity environments, like here on Earth, there is buoyant convection - warm, less dense air rises and cool dense air sinks. This creates a constant flow of air.

In a micro-gravity environment, like in The International Space Station (ISS), there is no natural convection. Air is very still if it is not forced to convection.

The space station Mir stank[1], but the ISS is smell-free due to an awesomely effective ventilation system.

---

[1] https://www.quora.com/How-do-farts-behave-in-low-gravity/answer/Iain-McClatchie

The Apollo 16

Fart fact # 62

The crew of the Apollo 16[1] were given potassium fortified citrus fruit drinks to avoid irregular heartbeats on their flight. That turned out to be a mistake.

The crew had chronic flatulence in their confined area with no air flow (like in the ISS) to help ventilate the smell.

The incident resulted in this loop call overheard by the ground: "I have the farts, again. I got them again, Charlie. I mean, I haven't eaten this much citrus fruit in 20 years! ...".

---

[1] http://www.popsci.com/nasas-uncensored-moonwalkers

The planet Venus

Fart fact number 63

No one would even notice a fart on Venus.

If the temperature on the surface of Venus were only 200 to 300 degrees Fahrenheit[1], liquid water could exist there because of the extremely high atmospheric pressure. But the temperature on Venus is almost 900 degrees Fahrenheit[2]. Humans are mostly water, and a person would actually become gas, like a whole-body fart! Still, the atmosphere on Venus already contains a lot of sulfur, so a fart, big or small, probably wouldn't even be noticed.

---

[1] 93 to 193 degrees Celsius.
[2] 482 degrees Celsius.

CHAPTER EIGHT

Farting Animals

Cattle

Fart fact # 64

Cattle fart. But for cattle, like most livestock, the vast majority of gas is not released from the back end, but from the front! In burps[1]. The amount of methane that one cow releases in a day is comparable to the amount of pollution produced by one car in a day!

Methane is one of the greenhouse gases that cause the greenhouse effect. Not difficult then to understand that agriculture is the main source of methane emissions globally[2].

---

[1]

http://animals.howstuffworks.com/mammals/methane-cow.htm

[2]

http://www3.epa.gov/climatechange/ghgemissions/gasses/ch4.html

Herring (fish)

Fart fact # 65

Some fish fart!

Biologists have been able to document that Herring fart[1]. The theory is that they do this to communicate after dark when they do not see each other.

But most fish probably do not fart. They do gulp air at the surface in order to fill their swim bladders and control buoyancy. If they have taken in too much air they will release it through their mouths. In burps!

---

[1] https://www.newscientist.com/article/dn4343-fish-farting-may-not-just-be-hot-air/

Turtles

Fart fact # 66

Turtles fart!

In 2009 an aquarium in Norfolk[1] had to release water from a turtle's tank. Farting from the turtle caused so much splashing in the tank that it triggered the overflow alarms!

---

[1]

http://www.dailytelegraph.com.au/news/weird/sprout-eating-turtle-farts-set-off-alarms/story-e6frev20-1225811490660

Snakes

Fart fact # 67

Snakes can fart!

Certain species can make loud farts[1] just like humans and usually when they feel threatened.

Some snakes and other reptiles have developed scent glands to protect themselves. This is not farting, but smells at least as bad when they release their smelly liquid when threatened.

---

[1] http://www.anapsid.org/snakefart.html

Termites

Fart fact # 68

Termites are the most notorious farters of all! Because of their diet of wood, termites are solely responsible for 11% of methane gas emissions globally.

Soldier termites can turn themselves into bombs! In order to protect themselves against ants they actually commit suicide by retracting muscles around a large gland that causes the gland to explode. They do this when in their nest to block tunnels up and prevent attackers (ants) from entering.

Beetles

Fart fact # 69

Beetles fart!

The female Southern Pine Beetle[1] farts a pheromone called *frontaline*. They can do this to attract a mate or use it as a gathering call when they need to defend themselves.

The Bombardier Beetle[2] can release a mixture of chemicals and enzymes that creates a puff of smoke and an audible popping sound when released! This astonishing fart is totally controlled by the beetle (otherwise it might accidentally blow up its rear end). The temperature of the explosive mixture is above boiling point of water. It serves as an effective defense mechanism.

---

[1]

http://www.spbinfodirect.ento.vt.edu/Chemecology/chemecol.html

[2] http://waynesword.palomar.edu/ww0502.htm

Blue whale

Fart fact # 70

Whales, dolphins and other marine mammals[1] are all known to fart. Just like people, gas is caused by their digestive system and by swallowing air.

A blue whale's fart bubbles are so large they can enclose a horse! It is said that they can last as long as one minute and that the forward thrust generated with each fart can propel the whale forward fifty feet[2]. And yes, they do stink. That's unbelievable!

---

[1] http://www.whalefacts.org/do-whales-fart/
[2] 15 meters

Non farting animals

Fart fact # 71

When a fart is defined to be an anal escape of intestinal gas, then it follows that animals that lack an anus cannot fart.

There are actually a few animals that lack an anus; some examples are sponges, cnidaria and pogonophoran worms.

Any creatures living very deep underwater probably don't fart. The high pressure causes gas to remain in solution and never emerges as bubbles, even though they possess intestines and anuses.

CHAPTER NINE

Famous Farts

The Norse God Thor

Fart fact # 72

In a popular mythological tale[1] about the great god Thor, a giant tricked him and he ended up spending a night in a mitten. According to the giant, Thor was so frightened that he "dared neither sneeze nor *fist*" (fart)!

---

[1] http://www.huffingtonpost.com/2012/07/30/the-word-fart-origins-etymology_n_1721585.html

1001 Arabian Night's Tales

Fart fact # 73

From one of the volumes of The Book of the Thousand Nights[1] it is written: "Abu Hasan, a former Badawi, wants to have a new wife after his former deceased. During the wedding celebration he lets off a great fart and flees out of shame to India. When he returns after ten years a mother still relates the case to her daughter upon which Abu flees again to India and remains and dies."

---

[1] https://1000into1night.wordpress.com/17-how-abu-hasan-brake-wind/

William Shakespeare

Fart fact # 74

One the greatest writers of all time, William Shakespeare, was a fan of fart jokes[1]!

One of Shakespeare's most famous fart references is from The Comedy of Errors: "A man may break a word with you, sir, and words are but wind / Ay, and break it in your face, so he break it not behind."
In other words, it's better to have someone break their word to you than fart.

There are plenty of fart jokes to be found in his plays, including some of his famous plays like Othello, King Lear and Henry IV.

---

[1]

https://shakesyear.wordpress.com/2011/02/03/blow-winds-and-crack-your-cheeks/#more-98

Dante Alighieri

Fart fact # 75

The major Italian poet Dante Alighieri writes in his 14th century masterpiece The Inferno about a demon that uses: "his ass as a trumpet!".

Benjamin Franklin

Fart fact # 76

Benjamin Franklin, while abroad as the first United States Ambassador to France, wrote an essay about farting called "Fart Proudly"!

The essay was not published.

James Joyce

Fart fact # 77

The famous Irish novelist James Joyce wrote about his wife[1] Nora:
"I think I would know Nora's fart anywhere. I think I could pick hers out in a roomful of farting women."

1

http://www.huffingtonpost.co.uk/2012/06/18/james-joyce-quotes-most-bizarre_n_1606120.html

Mark Twain

Fart fact # 78

The American author and humorist Marc Twain wrote in his one act-show 1601: "Nay tis not I [who has] brought forth this rich o'emastering [sic] fog, this fragrant gloom, so pray you seek ye further."

NASA Research

Fart fact # 79

Edwin L. Murphy and Doris H. Calloway[1], who were brilliant, ground-breaking nutritionists wrote a trilogy of flatulence-related papers that the pair worked on. The first published in 1968: "The Use of Expired Air to Measure Intestinal Gas Formation" and concluded in 1971 with: "Reduction of Intestinal Gas-Forming Properties of Legumes by Traditional and Experimental Food Processing Methods."

---

[1] http://io9.com/5876281/most-important-scientific-study-ever-what-about-farting-astronauts?trending_test_c&utm_expid=66866090-62._DVNDEZYQh2S4K00ZSnKcw.3&utm_referrer=http%3A%2F%2Fio9.com%2F5876281%2Fmost-important-scientific-study-ever-what-about-farting-astronauts

Disney

Fart fact # 80

   Disney has always been careful to maintain their family friendly image in anything associated with the Walt Disney brand. That's why it's notable that The Lion King featured *Pumbaa* (disney.wikia.com/wiki/Pumbaa) the warthog, the first Disney character farting[1]! No other Disney character had ever done such a thing on screen before.

---

[1]

http://entertainment.omgfacts.com/hollywood/39/8-Magical-Facts-You-Didn-t-Know-About-Disney-Films

J.D. Salinger

Fart fact # 81

The acclaimed American writer J.D. Salinger wrote in the very famous The Catcher in the Rye: "this guy sitting in the row in front of me, Edgar Marsalla, laid this terrific fart. It was a very crude thing to do, in the chapel and all, but it was also quite amusing. Old Marsalla. He damn near blew the roof off."

George Carlin

Fart fact # 82

In the 1970's the famous American stand-up comedian George Carlin (georgecarlin.com) added the word *fart* in continuation and expansion of his list of "Seven Words You Can Never Say on Television".

Siri

Fart fact # 83

If you own an iPhone and ask little know-it-all helper Siri[1] to play loud farts, she will try to play "What's My Name" by Rihanna featuring Drake.

---

[1] http://mashable.com/2015/07/13/siri-loud-farts/#IwUmf49BSiqI

CHAPTER TEN

Moneymaking Farts

5th century

Fart fact # 84

It's a rare talent, but some people are able to intentionally take air into their anus!
The first recorded fart performer entertained Augustine in the 5th century.

Since the air is sucked in from the outside, the farts are odorless.

Le Pétomane

Fart fact # 85

Le Pétomane (french for fartomaniac) was Joseph Pujol's (pronounced poo-hole) stage name. He was a 19th century performer capable of sucking in large quantities of air into his anus. He was even able to suck up an entire bowlful of water (just the water, not the bowl) and expel it again with considerable force.

He could perform lengthy shows on stage and could imitate musical instruments, farm animals and bird songs and even whistle melodies.

Le Pétomane performed for kings and queens.

Mr. Methane

Fart fact # 86

Mr. Methane "King of farts" claims being the world's only performing flatulist.

He also claims to have the record of the world's longest recorded fart (it's on YouTube).

There is a recording of Mr. Methane performing Let it Go from the movie Frozen (it's on YouTube).

Fart in a Jar

Fart fact # 87

    The unsuccessful project "Fart in a Jar" on Kickstarter tried to market farts from all over the globe: "Farts from 80 different nationalities have been collected for your sniffing pleasure."

Beano

Fart fact # 88

There is a pill for everything - even farting (or actually for trying to reduce farting).

Beano® cuts down on gas production by starving these bacteria.

The product prevents gas by breaking down complex carbohydrates found in many foods, making the foods easier to digest and by doing so avoiding that bacteria, which produces gas, is needed to break it down.

This is an over-the-counter product and it's proven to actually work.

Pilulepet

Fart fact # 89

On his website pilulepet.com (french for farting pill) a Frenchman has been selling pills since 2007 that he claims can make farts smell like chocolate, rose or ginger[1].

It is also possible to buy "fart powder for dogs that stink" on his website.

---

[1]

http://www.huffingtonpost.com/2014/11/26/christian-poincheval_n_6227404.html?ir=India&adsSiteOverride=in

Farty Pants

Fart fact # 90

There is a product called Farty Pants that sells underwear that actually absorbs the odor of farts. The product claims to be able to stop smells 200 times stronger than an average fart!

(Speaking of which, the 74th Emmy nominated episode of South Park was called "Osama bin Laden Has Farty Pants".)

Shreddies

Fart fact # 91

Another product called Shreddies offers not only underwear, but also pajamas and even jeans!

Snacks

Fart fact # 92

In 2001 an entrepreneur and food engineer named Kazemzadeh patented a "Process for producing reduced-flatulence, legume-based snack foods" (Google link).

Today however, he instead sells gluten-free products on his website kaysnaturals.com.

The Fart Blaster

Fart fact # 93

The Fart Blaster

The animation movie "Despicable Me 2" made the Fart Blaster "A Despicable Minion Gadget" become one of the hottest toys of 2013!

Professionals

Fart fact # 94

In China fart smelling is a profession[1] paying as much as $50,000!

"Professional gas smellers" claim to be able to tell a lot about a person's physical health.

---

[1] http://gizmodo.com/5966617/job-opportunity-how-about-an-exciting-career-as-a-professional-fart-smeller

A ruined career

Fart fact # 95

    In 2014, an opera singer with the Nashville Opera Company sued her hospital[1] over a botched medical procedure during the birth of her child that left her with excessive gas. According to the lawsuit, the singer alleged that she became unable to work as a professional opera singer as a result of excessive flatulence.

---

[1] http://www.huffingtonpost.com/2014/01/27/amy-herbst-farting-opera-singer_n_4674264.html

The Whoopie Cushion

Fart fact # 96

Probably the most popular inflatable toy ever! The whoopee cushion has been around since ancient Rome. The modern version of the cushion was re-invented in the 1920's by a Canadian company.

The world's largest working whoopee cushion measures an amazing 13 feet in diameter, is 15 feet long at nozzle and weighs 44lbs[1] (it's on YouTube).

---

[1] 3.9 meters in diameter, 4.6 meters long at nozzle and weights 20 kg.

CHAPTER ELEVEN

Farting Records

Loudest fart

Fart fact # 97

The loudest fart ever recorded took place in 1972 in Texas[1]. The record holder, Alvin Meshits, reached a level of 194 decibels for one third of a second!

---

[1] http://uncyclopedia.wikia.com/wiki/Fartium

Longest fart

Fart fact # 98

    Bernard Clemmens holds the official world record for the longest fart[1].
The guy from London managed to sustain a fart for 2 minutes and 42 seconds!

---

[1]

http://www.answers.com/Q/Who_has_the_longest_fart_in_the_world

Highest farting frequency

Fart fact # 99

The source is unknown and the record
unconfirmed, but the farting frequency record is said to
be 145 farts in 24 hours, 83 farts in 4 hours!

THAT'S IT

You can now claim to know at least 99 amazing,
awesome, fascinating and hilarious facts about farting!

Did you enjoy reading this book?
If so, please help spread the word
and leave a short review on Amazon.
Your review does make a difference.
Thank you!

Are you up for a challenge?
Get your FREE COPY of
"The Ultimate Quiz Book About Farts"
Visit: funfactbooks.com/free-quiz-book

Enjoy!

www.funfactbooks.com